DAILY LIFE IN A VICTORIAN HOUSE

Laura Wilson

HAMLYN

First published in Great Britain 1993
by Hamlyn Children's Books,
an imprint of Reed Children's Books,
Michelin House, 81 Fulham Road, London SW3 6RB,
and Auckland, Melbourne, Singapore and Toronto.
Reprinted in 1994

ISBN 0 600 57986 7

British Library Cataloguing-in-Publication Data
A catalogue record for this book is available from the
British Library.

Printed in Hong Kong

Conceived and produced by Breslich & Foss, London
Art Director: Nigel Osborne
Design: Sally Stockwell
Illustrations: Ben Warner, Deborah Gyan
Photography: Nigel Bradley

CONTENTS

THE VICTORIAN ERA

Victoria became queen on the death of her uncle, King William IV, in 1837. She was eighteen years old, and her Coronation took place a month after her nineteenth birthday. The tin mug shown on the right is a special souvenir of her Coronation. The lettering reads "Victoria crowned June 28th 1838". Her reign lasted sixty-four years, until her death, aged eighty-two, in 1901.

The British Empire

During the reign of Queen Victoria, the British Empire (that is, those countries which were colonized by Britain) grew larger than it had ever been before. Britain fought many wars to expand its territories and get new markets and sources for goods. Among its colonies were India, Egypt, and parts of Africa. Queen Victoria had a special interest in India and wanted to be proclaimed "Empress of India". Although many people were against this, she was given the title in 1876. On the right is a souvenir medal which was made for the occasion. "The scramble for Africa" took place between 1877 and 1914, when that continent was "discovered" by Europeans – France, Belgium, Germany, Portugal and Britain all had colonies there. Britain's colonies included the Gold Coast, Nigeria, Uganda, Kenya, Rhodesia (now Zimbabwe) and parts of South Africa. This led to wars between the previous European settlers of South Africa, known as "Boers", and the British in 1881 and from 1899 to 1902.

Money

Before Britain had decimal currency, the money was known as "l, s. and d.". These letters stand for the Latin words *librae*, *solidi* and *denarii*, meaning pounds, shillings and pence. There were 12d to one shilling (now 5p) and 20 shillings – or 240d – to £1. The smallest coin was a "farthing" which was worth a quarter of one penny. The bank notes were much bigger than modern ones – 20.7cm (8⅛") by 13.3cm (5¼"). They were made of white paper, with writing in black ink, and their values were £5, £10, £20, £100, £200, £300, £500 and £1000. During the 1870s and 1880s, £1 was worth £30 of today's money, so a £1,000 note was equivalent to £30,000!

Right: *This portrait was painted in 1846, and it shows Queen Victoria with Prince Albert, whom she married in 1840, and five of their children: from left to right, Alfred, Edward the Prince of Wales, Alice, Helena, and Vicky. There were four more to come: Louise, Arthur, Leopold and Beatrice.*

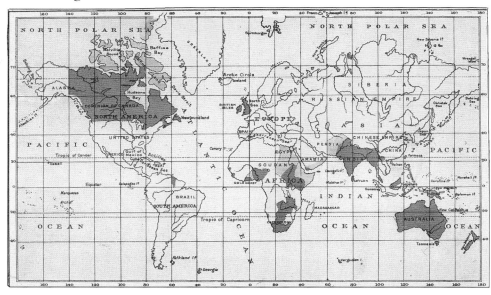

Above: *A map showing the extent of the empire c. 1880.*

Queen Victoria's reign was a time of peace and prosperity for Britain. The only two major wars of her reign, the Crimean War (1854-1856) and the Boer War (1899-1902) were fought far away from Britain, and, apart from the Indian Mutiny of 1857, even the conquest of the empire proceeded relatively peacefully. The Industrial Revolution, which began in the second half of the eighteenth century, was transforming people's lives with the invention of machines which made products quicker, better and on a larger scale than ever before. Industry grew, employment grew, overseas trade grew, and the country became more and more wealthy until, by mid-Victorian times, Britain was the greatest trading nation and the richest country in the world.

Railways played an important part in the Industrial Revolution. At first they were used only to carry coal, but by the 1840s Britain had a network of passenger railways,

Left: *Victorian coins.*

and by the end of the century over 20,000 miles of track had been laid. The steam trains that ran on these tracks were the first means of fast and cheap travel for everyone.

Right: *Benjamin Disraeli, Conservative Prime Minister in 1868, and from 1874 to 1880.*

As well as industrialization, many social changes took place in Victoria's reign. In the early 1800s, very few people were allowed to vote, but a series of "Reform Acts" gave the vote to more and more people – provided that they were men. Women were not allowed to vote at all.

Efforts were also made to improve the plight of the poor: although

Left: *William Gladstone, Liberal Prime Minister 1868 to 1874, 1880 to 1885, 1886, and 1892 to 1894.*

Britain was rich and prosperous, the wealth was not equally divided. The poorest people, with no job and no social security, were forced to go to the "Workhouse".

Workhouses gave people a roof over their heads and work, but families were split up and there was never enough food to go round – so that some people thought it better to starve in the streets.

THE FAMILY

The Smiths moved into their house (*see over*), in 1875, and they have lived there for several years. They are a middle class family. Mr Smith is a lawyer, and he earns around £2,000 a year, out of which he can afford to pay for four servants and a carriage with two horses. Like most middle class Victorians, the Smiths are very concerned about what people think of them, so they are careful to do everything "properly".

Above: *When bank holidays were introduced in 1871, family outings to the seaside became popular.*

For example, Mrs Smith never opens the front door to a guest or puts coal on the fire herself, she gets the maid to do it for her, in case people think she is "letting her husband down". The position of women in the last century was different from today: only poor women went out to work – wealthy ones like Mrs Smith stayed at home.

MR GEORGE SMITH

George Smith went to university before becoming a lawyer like his father. He met his wife Florence at a dance when he was twenty-five and they were married a year later. Florence's father is a doctor, so it was considered an excellent match by both families, who gave George some money to help with the cost of his new home. Mr Smith is the head of his family, and his word is law. Although he does not spend much time with his children, he is very fond of them, and takes an interest in their progress.

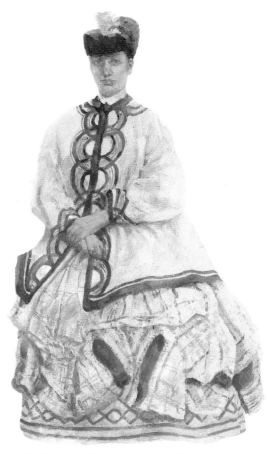

MRS GEORGE SMITH

Florence Kendall married George Smith when she was nineteen. They have three children – quite a small family by Victorian standards. There was a fourth child, a girl, but she died when she was only three months old. Mrs Smith takes great pride in her home and spends her days overseeing her servants, planning meals, paying calls on other ladies, shopping for clothes, seeing her dressmaker and sewing.

CHARLOTTE COOPER

Cook

Charlotte Cooper, like all cooks, has the title of "Mrs", even though she is not married – no-one would dare to call her Charlotte. She is forty years old, and earns £45 a year, as well as her meals and bed, because she is a "professed" cook. This means that she can make elaborate dinners and showy puddings as well as simple meals. "Plain" cooks, whose skills are more basic, earn less money. Thanks to Mrs Cooper, dinner parties at the Smiths' are always a success.

JANE DOBBS
&
MARY PARKER

Parlourmaid and Housemaid

Like most girls who are "in service", Jane and Mary both started work in their early teens. Now eighteen, Jane earns £16 a year as a parlourmaid and Mary, who is sixteen, earns £12 a year as housemaid. Jane and Mary have no time off work at all, except to go to church. This was true of almost all servants until the 1890s, when people began to give their staff one day off per month. By the 1900s, most servants were being allowed half a day off every week.

NURSE & CHILDREN

Ellen Stokes the nurse,
Albert Eustace (13), Alice Louise (6),
John Percival (3) and Bobby, the dog

The Smith's eldest son, Albert, was sent to a boarding school when he was ten. Alice and John are looked after by Ellen. When John gets older, he will also go to school, but Alice will be educated at home by a governess.

Ellen is thirty-five years old, earns £18 a year, and has worked for the Smiths ever since Albert was born. When she takes the children out for walks, Bobby comes with them.

LONDON LIFE

The Smiths live in a terraced house – that is, one of a row of houses joined together. It was built in 1873, and has four floors and a basement, and is made from yellow "London Stock" bricks, some of which are coated in white "stucco" plaster.

It is in a private road which is blocked off by gates, with a gatekeeper to let callers and tradesmen in, and refuse entry to "undesirables" such as beggars and street vendors. Behind the house is a garden and a mews with some stables,

Above: *By the mid-1850s, there were gas lamps like these in most towns and cities, and gas light was usual in middle and upper class houses.*

where the Smiths keep their carriage and horses. The house is situated in the fashionable "West End" of London, near parks, shops and theatres, and well away from smoky, noisy factories and railway lines. Most of the houses in this area are smart and well-kept, the people who live here usually have several servants, and many keep a carriage.

It is very different from the "East End", which is filthy, overcrowded and poverty-stricken. An 1865 report on the area found that it was "as unexplored as Timbuctoo": certainly, inhabitants of the West End like the Smiths are about as likely to venture into the East End as they are to go exploring in Darkest Africa.

During the 1880s and '90s, attempts were made to improve housing conditions in the East End, and provide the people with such services as public baths, parks and libraries. However, despite the Victorians' efforts, the East End remained a relatively poor area of London.

Right: *Poor people lived in slum houses. The landlords liked to squeeze as many people as possible into each house, so a lot of families ended up living in a single room. Tall slum buildings like these were called "rookeries".*

Poverty

One result of the Industrial Revolution was that more and more people left the countryside and came to live in the cities near the factories and workshops, and London was no exception to this. In the 1860s, the city's population was 3 million. By 1901, it had swollen to 4.5 million (Liverpool, Manchester and Birmingham, the next-largest cities, had populations of between 500,000 and 800,000).

A large number of these people were very poor. Many, like the "match girl" shown on page 8, scraped their living from selling things in the streets, rat catching, or even "mudlarking" – that is, searching in the mud beside the River Thames for any object which they could sell. Some people brought food scraps and used tea-leaves from rich people's kitchen doors and sold them to those with even less money than themselves, and others worked as "pure finders". These people collected dogs' mess and sold it to tanneries where it was used to darken the animal hides. Not surprisingly, some of these people turned to crime to keep themselves and their families fed and clothed.

Transport

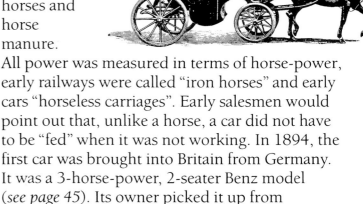

Despite the growth of the railways, Victorian society was still very dependent on the horse. Horses and ponies were everywhere, pulling carts and carriages, carrying loads and being ridden, and the air smelt strongly of horses and horse manure.

All power was measured in terms of horse-power, early railways were called "iron horses" and early cars "horseless carriages". Early salesmen would point out that, unlike a horse, a car did not have to be "fed" when it was not working. In 1894, the first car was brought into Britain from Germany. It was a 3-horse-power, 2-seater Benz model (*see page 45*). Its owner picked it up from the London docks and drove it to Charing Cross, where he was stopped by a policeman. The driver was breaking the law, because he had not got a man to walk along in front of the car so that people would know it was coming. Until the law was changed in 1896, all cars had to be preceded by a man on foot.

Below: *This is the entrance hall of the Smiths' house. On the next two pages, you can see the whole of the inside of the house.*

The Front

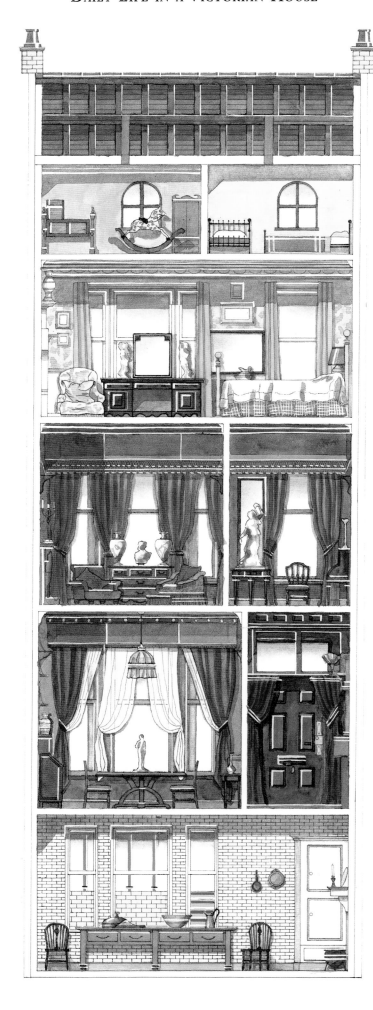

The Night Nursery:
Alice and John sleep here with Ellen, their nurse. Bobby the dog sleeps in a kennel in the garden.

The Master Bedroom:
This is where Mr and Mrs Smith sleep.

The Drawing Room:
This is where Mrs Smith entertains her friends to tea. Mr Smith comes in here after dinner to relax and smoke a cigar.

The Dining Room:
All Mr and Mrs Smith's meals are served in here. The servants eat downstairs, sitting round the kitchen table.

Jane and Mary share this attic bedroom. They do not have a wardrobe to hang their clothes in, so they keep them in tin trunks stowed under their beds. In Jane's previous job, or "situation" as it was called, she had been the only servant in the whole house, which was very lonely. So, although their little room is cramped, she values Mary's company.

The front door and hall: *Mrs Smith chose a patterned wallpaper for the hall, and decorated the walls with glass cases of stuffed birds and fish, and two stags' heads with antlers, mounted on wooden shields.*

The Kitchen (front):
Outside the kitchen is the little yard known as the "area", with a flight of steps leading up to the street.

The Back

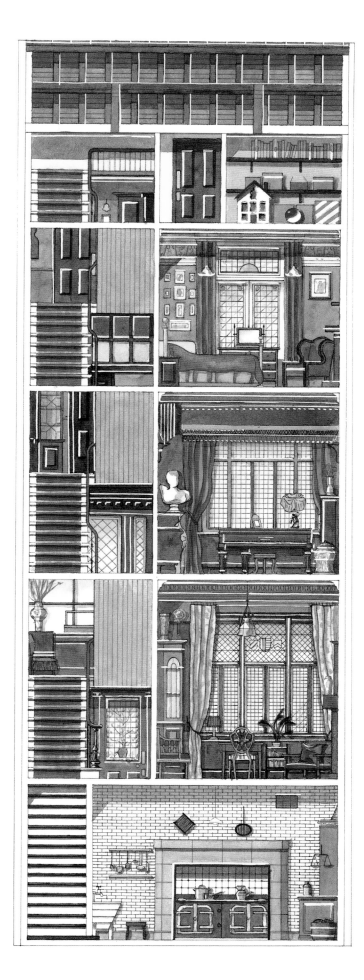

The door leads to Mrs Cooper's bedroom. As she is the most important servant, her bedroom is much nicer than the maids' room.

The door on the landing leads to the Smiths' bathroom.

The back door leads into the garden and the mews where the Smiths' carriage is kept.

As these stairs are used only by the servants (Mrs Smith hardly ever comes down to the kitchen), they do not have carpet.

The Day Nursery: *During the day, Alice and John play in here, watched over by Ellen.*

The Guest Room: *If the Smiths have any people to stay, they sleep in this bedroom. When Albert is home from his boarding school, he sleeps here.*

The Drawing Room (back) *with the piano.*

The Parlour: *Mrs Smith sits in here in the mornings, doing her sewing. Mrs Cooper, wearing a clean apron, comes up to discuss the day's meals with her.*

The Kitchen (back): *Mrs Cooper does all her cooking on the range set into the wall, and Mary washes up in the wooden sink. The floor is made of grey stone slabs called "flagstones".*

EARLY MORNING

S ervants' days were long: at work by 6am, they might not get to bed until midnight, or later if their employers had given a dinner party or gone to a ball. People like the Smiths thought that they had bought every moment of their servants' time except "what God and nature required".

Left: *With no radio or television, newspapers and magazines are the main source of information. The* Times, *whose first edition was on January 1st 1785, is one of the most respectable papers, and is taken up to Mr Smith every morning with his tea. Some employers insist that their servants iron the pages to make them perfectly smooth, but Mr Smith does not mind if his paper is a little creased.*

First Duties

Mary's first job of the day is to light the fire in the kitchen range so that Mrs Cooper can make the tea and start cooking the Smiths' breakfast. She then attends to the front door and steps (*see below*) before dusting the parlour and doing the fire. Then she takes coal upstairs to the nursery for Ellen and cleans Mr Smith's shoes. After that, she carries cans of hot water up to Mr Smith's room so that he can shave. Jane opens the shutters in the lower rooms, and does their fires. After that, she sprinkles the carpets with damp tea leaves to lay the dust before brushing them thoroughly. She lays the table in the dining room for breakfast, and then, at 7am, takes the tea tray upstairs for Mrs Smith and helps her to get dressed. She has to change into a clean apron and wash her hands first – otherwise she might get coal on Mrs Smith's clothes.

"At six o'clock every morning I have to clean the brass on the front door. Then I sweep the doorstep and trudge back down to the area for cold water and a scrubbing brush. On a dark winter morning, doing the steps is not a job I enjoy." Mary Parker

Above: *During the winter, when fires are lit, this black-lead is used daily to make the grates shiny. For the summer, Mary and Jane paint the grates with a home-made varnish of "common asphaltum" mixed with linseed and turpentine.*

Coal Fires

Victorian houses had no central heating, and keeping them warm in winter used up a lot of coal. Around half a million people worked in mines, extracting the coal needed to heat homes and fuel factories and trains. Until 1842, women and children also worked in the mines – thirteen hour days were common even though some children were under seven years old.

Smoke pollution was very bad in large towns. The sulphur puffed out by coal fires caused smogs or "pea-soupers" – so-called because the fog was yellow. If you were caught in a fog, it was impossible to see more than a couple of inches in front of you. A bad one might last for days and fill all the houses with a smoky haze and a horrible smell. These smogs continued in Britain until 1956, when a law was passed making it illegal to burn coal in cities.

"Sometimes the fire won't light. It almost makes me weep in frustration – there is so much to do before breakfast." Jane Dobbs

Left: *Coal has to be added to keep the fire burning. Extra coal is put in a coal-scuttle like this.*

Right: *Mary and Jane each have a "maid's box" where they keep the things they need to clean and polish the grates – brushes, cloths, emery papers and black-lead. They take their boxes from room to room as they work.*

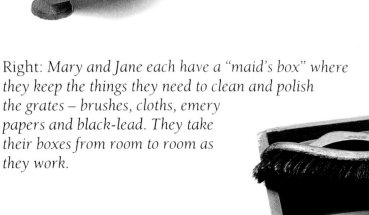

DRESSING MRS SMITH

Mrs Smith decides which clothes she will wear. Jane lays them out for her, and stands by to lace her corsets and help her on with her bustle (*see below*).

Today it is fashionable to be slim, and many women diet and exercise in order to keep their figures. Victorian women did neither. Instead, they moulded their figures into a fashionable shape with the help of corsets and padding. The ideal shape changed from the "bell" of the crinoline to the "S" shape of the bustle during the last half of the nineteenth century, but at no time did skirts rise above the ankle. Other unchanging rules were that hats or bonnets were always worn out of doors and sleeveless dresses were never worn during the day.

Above and left: *A lady's underwear – corset, chemise, bustle and drawers.*

The dress shown on the right has a separate bodice fastened by twenty-two buttons and a waistband. The skirt is so heavy that braces have to be worn under the bodice to hold it up. The bustle at the back is typical of the style worn in the 1880s. Wire cages, horse hair pads and even crumpled newspaper were all used to make bustles.

"It would be impossible to be seen downstairs in my dressing gown. I change my clothes three time a day, and really, it keeps my maid and myself extraordinarily busy."
Florence Smith

Above: *A velvet and satin dress with a bustle and handmade lace trimmings.*

Right: *Stockings had embroidery only on the instep and ankle, where it would be seen.*

Make-Up and Hairstyles

Victorian ladies did not wear any make-up because it was not considered respectable. It was fashionable for ladies to look sweet and demure, and the ideal of beauty was to be "pale and interesting". A very white skin could be achieved by drinking vinegar and some ladies even drank small amounts of arsenic. The most popular hairstyle was a middle parting with ringlets on either side (*shown left*). By the end of the century, companies such as the soap manufacturer Pears were using famous faces like the actress Lillie Langtry and the singer Adelina Patti to advertise their products, and cosmetics companies soon followed their lead.

Changing Fashions

There were two important reasons why fashions changed more quickly in the nineteenth century than ever before. The first was the rise in the number of people who could read. Magazines and newspapers printed information about the latest trends, and women were quick to follow them. The second was the development in the 1840s of the "mechanical tailor" or sewing machine. By the end of the 1860s, traditional hand sewing was replaced almost entirely by machine. However, compared to modern clothes, few of the designs were very practical. This was because the ideal Victorian lady was "helpless" and had to be looked after by others.

Above and left: *A silk day dress from the early 1860s and the crinoline worn beneath it.*

Right: *Parasols shaded ladies' faces from the sun and stopped them getting freckles or – worse – a tan.*

Accessories

Victorian ladies had many accessories: bags, fans, gloves, mittens, parasols and hats. Hats were often very elaborate, with artificial flowers, lace, ostrich feathers and even whole stuffed birds. In the last half of the nineteenth century, they became more fashionable than bonnets, despite the fact that Queen Victoria preferred bonnets and continued to wear them. Gloves were always worn out of doors and kept stretched with special "glove-stretchers" made of wood, bone or brass so that they fitted well.

MR SMITH'S CLOTHES

The perfect Victorian man was a husband and father who was head of his family. He provided for and protected his wife and children, who had to do whatever he told them. Before the Victorian era, fashionable men's clothes had often been made in bright colours, with plenty of embroidery and lace trimmings. Men had worn shoes with high heels and big buckles. But these fancy things were not serious enough for a Victorian man like Mr Smith. His suits, which consist of a frock coat and a pair of striped or plaid trousers, are made of dark cloth.

Above: *Some men went to a barber's shop for a shave, but many shaved at home – an easy task for the few who had hot running water.*

Below: *Every gentleman's wardrobe had to include a top hat. Jane steams and brushes Mr Smith's hat regularly to keep it looking smart.*

Above: *Beards, moustaches and side-whiskers were all popular as they were thought to look manly.*

Above: *Cut-throat razors like the one on the right were used (see page 45).*

Above: *Toothpaste was sold in china pots.*

There is one patch of colour in Mr Smith's sombre outfit – his waistcoat. Waistcoats are made in colourful, patterned fabrics. Tartan was especially popular. It had become fashionable when Queen Victoria and Prince Albert bought Balmoral Castle in Scotland in 1844, and started spending their holidays there. Albert and the children frequently dressed in tartan, and the queen had her photograph taken dressed as a Highland wife with a tartan shawl.

MOURNING

I n 1861, Prince Albert died. Although Queen Victoria was only 42, she remained in mourning for the rest of her life – 40 years. Her example was copied by many Victorian women, and there were very strict rules about clothes and behaviour. The customs of mourning did not affect men as much as women; men only had to wear a black armband.

Left: *Jet jewellery and hair ornaments were very popular.*

If Mr Smith died, Mrs Smith would have to go into "deep mourning" for at least a year afterwards. This would mean that she had to wear black and only leave her house to visit close relatives or go to church. In the second year, she would be able to go out to close friends' houses. In the third year, she could start wearing the "half-mourning" colours of grey, white and purple.

Funerals

Rich people's funerals were expensive. The black horses which pulled the hearse had a black harness trimmed with silver, and black feathers on their heads. "Feathermen" carried trays of ostrich plumes in front of the hearse. The "mutes" who walked with them were men who were specially chosen for their glum faces. They wore black coats, top hats and sashes. The family of the dead person gave the mourners special gloves and scarves to wear. They might also give necklaces or bracelets made with the dead person's hair as a keepsake.

The greatest shame for a poor person was to be given a "pauper's burial" because it meant that their family could not afford a decent funeral. Some families paid in money to a "burial club" each week to make sure they could afford a horse-drawn hearse when they died. The poor had to be buried on Sunday – the only day they did not have to work. However, if a family had not saved enough money to hold the funeral on the first Sunday after death, the corpse would have to stay in the (usually crowded) house for a whole week, during which the family might have to go without food to save up the money.

Right: *The death of babies and young children was much more common than it is today.*

Left: *Queen Victoria's daughters in mourning for their father. After his death, a marble bust of Prince Albert was always given a central place in the royal family's photographs.*

BREAKFAST

Victorian breakfasts were big meals. Cold meat might be served, or game pie, alongside a selection of hot dishes such as mutton chops, rumpsteak, and kidneys, as well as bacon and eggs. There was also toast and marmalade, English muffins and tea, coffee and cocoa to drink.

Above: *"Meat safes" like this one protected meat from flies.*

Preserving Food

Early refrigerators or "ice-safes", like the one on the left, were large wooden chests lined with zinc, with a big lump of ice inside to keep the food cool and fresh. They could only be opened once a day in case the ice melted and caused a flood. Like most Victorian houses, the Smiths' home does not have a refrigerator. Instead, Mrs Cooper inspects the meat and dairy produce each day to make sure it is still fresh.

Food was first put in tins in the early nineteenth century, when it was given to sailors for long voyages. By the late 1870s, tinned food had become popular with everyone.

The Smiths have breakfast at half-past eight. Before breakfast, the family and servants gather in the dining room for prayers. Then Ellen takes the children back to the nursery and Mrs Cooper rushes off to finish her cooking. Jane brings up the Smiths' hot food and drinks and Mary takes the children's food to the nursery.

What was eaten depended on what was in season at the time. For example, apples were not available in the summer, so if you wanted apple pie, you would have to wait until October when they were ripe.

Left: *Kedgeree, grilled sheep's kidneys and toast.*

Book Keeping

Mr Smith goes to his office after breakfast, and Mrs Smith does the household accounts. She writes down how much is spent on each item. Mrs Smith trusts Mrs Cooper with the shopping but her former cook was not so honest – she would buy cheap food and say that it was expensive, so that she could keep the extra money.

Above: *Mrs Smith does her accounts in the parlour.*

Tradesmen

Mrs Cooper buys food from tradesmen who come to call at the kitchen door. The butcher, baker and greengrocer call daily. Tradesmen like these keep a horse and cart to take their wares from house to house, and the milkman has a little chariot drawn by a pony, with two big churns on it. He measures out Mrs Cooper's milk in a jug. Other tradesmen, such as the coalman and the chimney sweep, also call regularly. Like many other maids, this is Jane and Mary's only chance to meet young men. Mary is shy, but Jane enjoys chatting to the handsome butcher's boy until Mrs Cooper comes and shooes her back into the house.

19

CLEANING THE HOUSE

The Victorians thought that "Cleanliness is next to Godliness" and demanded high standards from their servants. However, houses like the Smiths' are hard to keep clean. The coal fires, candles and oil-lamps cover the house with a layer of soot that Jane and Mary have to clean off every day.

Above: *The Smiths' house has six flights of stairs like this one, and all the carpets have to be brushed and the brass stair-rods taken up and polished every week.*

Above: *Mary and Jane keep the silver shiny with a home-made polish of "hartshorn" powder, which contains ammonia and alcohol.*

The Smiths, like other Victorian home-owners, like to cover every single surface with ornaments and every inch of wall with pictures, which means that Jane and Mary have lots of dusting to do. They also have wooden floors and furniture to polish, carpets to brush and cabinets full of glass and china to keep washed and polished. All the rooms are thoroughly cleaned at least once a week, and Mary scrubs the wooden draining boards and the stone floor of the kitchen and the front steps of the house every morning.

Endless kneeling meant that many servants like Jane and Mary suffered from "housemaid's knee". They had no rubber gloves to protect their hands, and constant contact with cold water and harsh soap and soda crystals made them raw and painful – there was no question of buying hand-cream, which was an expensive luxury for rich ladies.

"After breakfast, it's back to the scrubbing brush again… I get a handful of soda to put in the water and household soap which comes in bars about a foot long, a nasty mustard in colour and very harsh on my poor broken-skinned hands…"
Mary Parker

Knife Cleaning

Before stainless steel, knives had to be specially cleaned to stop them rusting. The machine on the left could clean two knives at once: they were pushed into the slots at the top.

Above: *Knife cleaning powder. Mary pours this into the hole in the side of the machine and turns the handle to make the brushes and pads clean the knives.*

Below: *Victorian feather dusters were made with real feathers.*

Carpet Sweepers

Although servants were constantly cleaning, their old-fashioned methods meant that quite a lot of the dust was simply moved around the house rather than taken away. The Victorians were great inventors, but they had few of the cleaning appliances which are so familiar today. In the 1870s, an American called Melville Bissell invented a machine he called a "carpet sweeper". It was a revolving brush on wheels, pushed over the carpets with a long handle. It was very popular with servants because it meant that they did not have to get down on their knees to sweep the carpet, but it was not very good at getting rid of all the dust.

Vacuum Cleaners

The vacuum cleaner or "hoover" was invented in 1899. The early models were huge and drawn by horses, rather like Victorian fire-engines. If you wanted your house vacuumed, you ordered the cleaner and the driver stopped the horses outside your door. The hoses were passed into the house through the windows, and the operators attached nozzles to the tubes to vacuum out the dirt. This was such a novelty that people would ask their friends around to drink tea and watch the cleaners at work! "Portable" machines like the one below were not available until the early 1900s. At first, home-owners refused to buy them, saying that they did not need an expensive machine when their servants could do the work. However, after World War I ended in 1918, it became difficult for people to get staff. Many would-be employers tried to tempt servants to work for them by promising to buy a vacuum cleaner to make their chores easier.

Right: *Portable vacuum cleaner, c.1910.*

THE KITCHEN

The Smiths' kitchen is in the basement of the house. It can be reached from the outside by a separate flight of steps, which is the servants' and tradesmen's entrance. Only the Smiths and their friends may use the front door. The basement rooms are very dark, because only a small amount of light manages to filter through the space between the steps and the house, which is called the "area", and fenced off with iron railings.

The kitchen has a flagstone floor, a large wooden table and a coal-fired range where all the cooking is done. It has to be cleaned and lit by six o'clock every morning. The kitchen is Mrs Cooper's kingdom, and woe betide Jane and Mary if they do not obey her orders. Mrs Smith never sets foot "below stairs". If she was to come into the kitchen, or try to tell Mrs Cooper how to do her shopping, the cook would think that she was a busybody, and not a "nice lady".

Left: *Copper pan.*

Above: *A cooking range with copper pots.*

Above Left: *Few items were pre-packed. Sugar came in "cones" like this one. When Mrs Cooper wants sugar, she snips some off the top with special "cutters".*

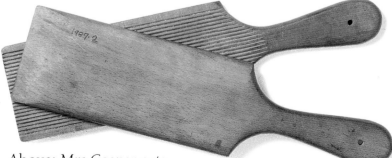

Above: *Mrs Cooper cuts pieces off a big lump of butter and uses these wooden "butter hands" to shape them into neat squares.*

Above: *Mixing bowls were wooden.*

PIG'S TROTTERS

This recipe comes from Mrs Beeton's Book of Household Management. *Mrs Beeton refers to pig's trotters as "pettitoes".*

Ingredients:
Pig's trotters, heart and liver, 1 thin slice of bacon, 1 onion, 1 blade of mace, 6 peppercorns, 3 or 4 sprigs of thyme, 1 pint of gravy, pepper and salt to taste, thickening of butter and flour.

Method:
Put the liver, heart and trotters into a stew-pan with the bacon, mace, peppercorns, thyme, onion and gravy, and simmer gently for ¼ hour. Take out the heart and liver and mince them finely. Keep stewing the trotters until quite tender, then return the minced parts, thicken the gravy with a little butter and flour, add the seasoning, and simmer gently for five minutes. Dish the mince, split the trotters, and arrange them on a dish with snippets of toast. Pour the gravy into the middle.

"I run and hide if I ever upset any milk or gravy. Mrs Cooper's rage has to be seen to be believed."
Mary Parker

Water

The Smiths' kitchen has a shallow stone sink and a cold water tap. This was quite a luxury – if you lived in a slum, you might have to share the cold tap in the yard with as many as fifty others. Piped water was not always very clean, and anyone who could afford it had a water filter. However, many people died of cholera, which they caught from drinking polluted water. There was no way of having hot water on tap, so all the water for cooking, washing-up and bathing had to be heated over the fire in the kitchen.

It was also impossible to get rid of rubbish down the sink. It was usually thrown on the fire. Fortunately, most of it would burn – there was no plastic or styrofoam packaging.

Inventions

Mincing machines were first made in 1853. Cooks did not like to waste anything, so they put all the scraps through the mincer to make a meat paste which could be sealed in pots and kept for a long time. By the 1890s, most cooks had egg-whisks, cream-whippers and food-slicers as well.

Left: *Mrs Cooper keeps spices such as nutmeg, cinnamon and allspice (pimento) in boxes like these.*

Below: *By 1900, there were many hand-operated machines like this one for chopping, mincing and slicing food.*

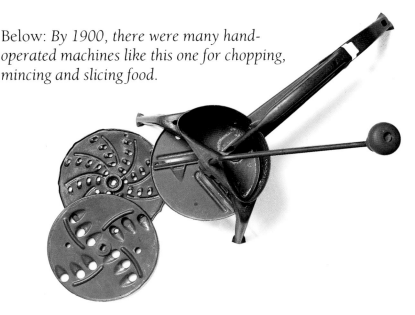

23

Left: *Mrs Smith has luncheon in the dining room and the children eat in the nursery. When Mr Smith is at work, he lunches at his club.*

Right: *Staple foods – cabbage, potatoes, onions, meat and fish. Meat was thought to be more nourishing than fish.*

LUNCHEON

S mart people called their midday meal "luncheon", but their servants called it "dinner". Cold meat or chops were often served. If there was a big joint of meat, it was first sent upstairs for the mistress' lunch and then finished by the servants. Servants were often better fed than other working class people (see page 25) because they had free meals, and, if their employers were not mean, that meant a diet of high-quality food. However, sometimes the mistress spent part of her housekeeping money on clothes for herself, so she would try to balance the books by keeping the servants on short rations. The Smiths' servants think they are lucky, as Mrs Smith always makes sure they have enough food, and does not lock away the tea, sugar, jam and eggs like some ladies.

Left: *Sticky "flypapers" like this one were hung from pantry ceilings. At the end of a summer day, they would be black with struggling, buzzing flies that had got stuck to the paper.*

24

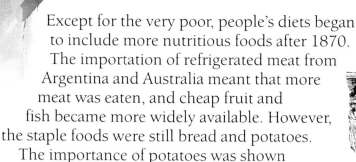

Except for the very poor, people's diets began to include more nutritious foods after 1870. The importation of refrigerated meat from Argentina and Australia meant that more meat was eaten, and cheap fruit and fish became more widely available. However, the staple foods were still bread and potatoes. The importance of potatoes was shown during the potato famine in Ireland in the 1840s. The crops failed because of a blight, or disease, and over a million people died. To escape starvation, many Irish people emigrated to the United States.

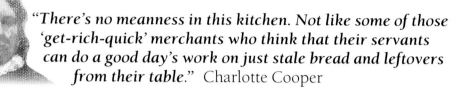

"There's no meanness in this kitchen. Not like some of those 'get-rich-quick' merchants who think that their servants can do a good day's work on just stale bread and leftovers from their table." Charlotte Cooper

The family of a low-paid man such as a farm-worker had to exist on bread, potatoes and tea, with meat or eggs perhaps once a week. A skilled worker, such as an engineer (who might earn three times as much as a farm-worker) could afford to feed his family better. They might have meat every day, and their diet would also include fruit, pastries, coffee and jam. Fish and chips, which was "invented" in Lancashire, was a favourite supper. Many people suffered illnesses caused either by bad food, or lack of food. One of the reasons that people today are generally taller, stronger and healthier than they were a hundred years ago is that they have a better, more balanced diet.

Right: *Big cooked meals meant lots of greasy plates to wash. Suet puddings were popular, and the cloths in which they were boiled had to be washed – not easy with no hot running water or detergent.*

THE NURSERY

I f the kitchen is Mrs Cooper's kingdom, then the nursery belongs to Ellen, or "Nurse Stokes", as she is known to everyone. She has complete control over Alice Louise and John Percival. Except for morning prayers and the hour spent in the drawing room with Mrs Smith, John and Alice rarely see their parents. All their meals are taken in the nursery and Mr and Mrs Smith are not encouraged to come up and see them – especially Mr Smith, who is inclined to romp with them. If Mrs Smith is not entertaining or paying calls, she sometimes looks in on their tea. Alice and John love Ellen very much – she reads them stories, looks after them when they are ill, and comforts them when they are unhappy. They tell her secrets that they would not dream of telling their parents.

Above: *This cradle is made of cane. It could be rocked to lull the baby to sleep. Behind the cradle is a homemade "scrap-screen".*

Above:
A baby's bib
and china feeding bottle.

"I love Mama, of course I do, but she does not bath me or brush my hair. Nurse Stokes does that, and I love her, too, but it's different."
Alice Louise Smith

The Nanny

Often a nanny would stay with one family for her whole working life, looking after several generations of children. It was usual for nannies to start as nursemaids, stepping into the nanny's shoes when she retired. Ellen does not have a nursemaid to help her, so she has to clean the nursery and fetch the bathwater herself. Alice and John are lucky, because Ellen is kind and gentle, unlike some nannies who are cruel or careless. However, Ellen is very firm, and she makes sure that Alice and John follow a strict routine: after breakfast, they go for a walk in the park. Some nannies meet their boyfriends in the park, and bully or bribe the children not to tell their parents. Ellen never does that but she enjoys chatting to other nannies while the children play. The rest of the day is spent in the nursery, playing and doing simple lessons. Alice and John have a rest after lunch, and then play until tea-time. After tea, Ellen puts on their smart clothes and combs their hair before taking them downstairs to see Mrs Smith at five o'clock. Afterwards Ellen baths them, and they say a prayer together: "Jesus, tender shepherd, hear me, Bless Thy little lambs tonight, Through the darkness be Thou near me, Keep me safe till morning light." They are in bed by half-past six. Ellen sleeps in the night nursery with them.

Above:
This dress belongs to John. Very young boys wore dresses and pantaloons.

Pets

Alice and John are very fond of the family spaniel, Bobby. Dogs, especially spaniels and pugs, were popular pets in the Victorian era. The queen herself kept many dogs, and had fond memories of her first dog, a spaniel called Dash. She had her portrait painted with him when she was 11 years old. Cats were kept in the kitchen, to keep down the mice.

Poor Children

Victorian families were much larger than modern ones – it was quite usual to have five children, and some people had as many as twelve.

For the poor, the more children they had, the less food there was to go round, and children were often hungry, cold and neglected by parents who had to work long hours for a tiny wage. There were no social security payments to help them, so the children were sent out to work as soon as they were old enough. Many worked in factories, where frequent accidents were caused by exhausted children falling into machinery. The parents got no compensation money if their children died from injuries.

Two acts of parliament were passed to improve their lot: the 1847 "Ten Hours" Act which limited working time per day (although ten hours is at least three hours more than the modern school day). There was also the 1870 Act which made it a law that children had to attend school. However, many had to work after school, because their families would have starved otherwise.

Schools called "Board Schools" were set up for these children, but the education was not very good. With as many as 70 pupils to a class, the single teacher spent more time keeping order than actually teaching.

Right: *Alice and John wore shoes and socks, but many children had to go barefoot, even in the winter.*

27

TOYS AND GAMES

Right: A toy theatre with cardboard characters and a play to perform.

Well-to-do children in the nineteenth century had more toys than ever before, including musical boxes, toy soldiers, educational board games and train sets, which appeared shortly after the introduction of railways in the 1820s and '30s. There were also magic lanterns and optical toys, such as the "phenakistoscope" on page 29. These were simple gadgets which gave the illusion of moving pictures. They were the forerunners of cinema. In the early years, cinema programmes often included lantern shows as well as short films. One toy that Victorian children did not have was the teddy bear. Named after the American President Theodore "Teddy" Roosevelt, the first teddy bears appeared in 1903.

Left: This doll's head, arms and legs are made of a porcelain called "bisque". Her body is fabric stuffed with sawdust.

Left: Early dolls looked more grown-up than the later child-like ones which children preferred.

Right: Most Victorian doll's houses were modelled on middle-class homes, but they often had old-fashioned furniture like four-poster beds. Shops and market stalls with miniature goods were also made.

Left: *The nanny gave the young children simple lessons. Older girls were taught by a governess who lived in the family house, and boys went to school.*

Below: *The rocking horse, always dapple-grey, with a real horse-hair mane and tail, was one of the most popular toys.*

Right: *Noah's ark was one toy which could be played with on Sundays because it was Biblical.*

Children's Books

Victorian children's books were frequently full of warnings to their readers about the terrible things that would happen to them if they were naughty. The most famous of these was the *Struwwlpeter*, which contained the story of Harriet who burnt to death because she played with matches, Augustus who died because he would not eat up his soup and "naughty little Suck-a-thumb" whose thumbs were cut off by a "great, long red-legg'd scissor man". However, some books were less severe – there were pop-up books, fairy tales and adventure stories. The Smith children like to read, and their favourite books are still read today: *Alice's Adventures in Wonderland* by Lewis Carroll, the tales of Hans Christian Andersen, *Little Women* by Louisa M. Alcott and *Black Beauty* by Anna Sewell. Children's books had beautiful pictures, sometimes in colour, and their illustrators, like Kate Greenaway, are still popular.

Below: *When the figures on this "phenakistoscope" are whirled around, they seem to be moving.*

THE LAUNDRY

The Smiths send their dirty clothes to a laundry to be washed. They are collected on Mondays and returned on Thursdays, ready to wear. Laundry was very hard work because many clothes were trimmed with ribbons and lace which had to be taken off before washing, and sewn back on afterwards. Even the buttons had to be removed in case they were broken in the mangle.

Women from poor families did their own washing – even if they got up at dawn to light the fires to heat water, the family's weekly wash still took a whole day. Traditionally, wash day was Monday.

Above: *Mangles squeezed water out of the clothes to help them dry, and smoothed them flat.*

Left: *The washerwoman's job was exhausting. She had no rubber gloves, so the water was as hot as her hands could bear.*

Right: *Linen presses kept table cloths and sheets smooth and flat until they were needed.*

Washing

After soaking the clothes in hot soapy water to loosen the dirt, the washerwoman had to rub them hard to remove any stains. Before the invention of washing machines, all this was done by hand, with the help of a "dolly" or "posser" and a washboard (*both shown left*). The dolly, possibly named because it looked like a simple doll with "arms" and "legs", was used for pounding the clothes as they soaked in a hot tub. The washerwoman held the arms of the dolly and thumped it down on the clothes until they were clean. The washboard was made from corrugated iron or zinc. The washerwoman would soap the clothes and rub them against the ridged board to get rid of the dirt. Instead of washing powder, the Victorians had soda crystals and yellow soap. Very dirty clothes were soaked in lime and water.

Early washing machines, such as those displayed at the Great Exhibition of 1851, were little more than tubs with paddles inside them. The tub was filled with hot suds, the clothes put in and the handle turned to make the paddles spin round. They often ripped the clothes they were supposed to wash.

Ironing

Once the clothes were starched and dried, they were ready for ironing. Before electricity, irons had to be heated up by the fire. The laundress tested them with her hand or spat on them to see if they were hot enough to use. As she worked, her iron would cool down and have to be returned to the fire again. She had to check the base of the iron for soot, or it would leave smudges on the clean clothes.

Different kinds of irons were used: the flat-iron; the box-iron, which was the first self-heating model; and the goffering iron for pleats and frills. They were very heavy. A large iron might weigh 10lbs – ten times as much as a modern one. Electric irons were invented in 1882. They were very dangerous – users spoke of weird noises, blinding light and flying sparks. Safer electric irons were first sold in America in 1904.

Above: *Flat-irons like these small ones were the most commonly used. When not in use, they were rested on trivets like these to keep them clean. The large iron is a box-iron* (see below). *The pegs were made of wood.*

Right: *Box-irons were filled with hot coals or lumps of hot iron.*

Left: *When the iron was heated, the handle became red hot. Even with a cloth, like the one shown here, placed over the handle, laundry maids often burned themselves.*

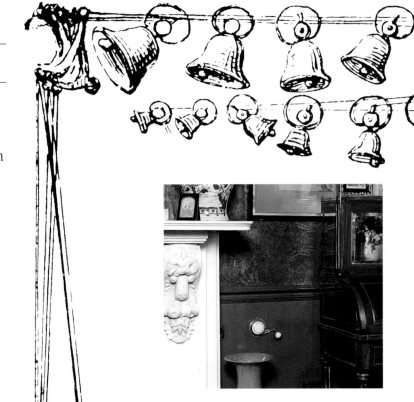

PAYING A CALL

Victorian ladies had complicated rules of "etiquette" or proper social behaviour. If Mrs Smith wanted to make friends with a lady called Mrs Brown, she would go to Mrs Brown's house and give the parlourmaid a card with her name and address on it. When Mrs Brown got the card, she would ask her friends if they knew Mrs Smith, and if she was a nice lady. If everyone agreed that Mrs Smith was charming, Mrs Brown would go to Mrs Smith's house and leave her own card. Then Mrs Smith would know that Mrs Brown wanted to meet her, and she would call at Mrs Brown's and have tea. Mrs Smith and Mrs Brown could then become friends. However, if a lady decided that she did not want to "know" another lady, she would tell her parlourmaid to say that she was "not at home". Another way to make this clear was to return a call by only leaving a card at the caller's house. As it was proper to repay a call with a call and a card with a card, the lady would know that she had been snubbed. Books and magazines advised ladies never to take their dogs when they went calling, or their children, unless they were "particularly well-trained and orderly".

Left: *Visitors were offered tea with cake or biscuits, served on the best china.*

32

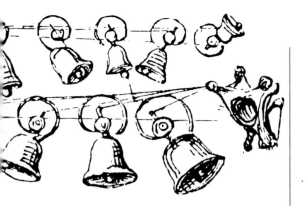

The Smiths could afford a doctor. Those who could not had no treatment. Despite improvements in medicine, diseases like influenza and tuberculosis killed millions. There were many other hazards: women often died in childbirth, and ignorance about chemicals made some jobs very risky. For example, the mercury used to make felt hats caused brain damage – which is why we say that a person is as "mad as a hatter".

Above and Left: If Mrs Smith wants anything, she turns this handle (left). A bell rings in the kitchen, and Jane goes up to find out what she wants. Each bell was labelled, so the servants would know which room to attend.

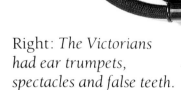

Right: *The Victorians had ear trumpets, spectacles and false teeth. In the previous century, false teeth were made from real teeth – Victorian ones were made of ivory.*

Left: *A portable medical case.*

In the early nineteenth century hospitals were dirty, and surgeons did not clean their instruments or change their bloodstained aprons. They did not know that they were spreading germs and causing the infections that killed most of their patients. When the French chemist Louis Pasteur published his "germ theory" of disease in 1865, the doctors who followed his advice about hygiene found that many more of their patients were getting well. In 1847, it was discovered that chloroform could be used to put patients to sleep during operations. Previously, patients were simply blindfolded and tied down for surgery, and often died from pain and shock.

Right: *Early syringe.*

Left: *Victorian houses were full of clutter. Obsessed by "things", the Victorians flocked to see the Great Exhibition of 1851 with its show of ornaments, bric-à-brac and gadgets. People like the Smiths displayed everything they owned from fine china to photographs and knick-knacks. This was a sign that they were well-off and respectable.*

Florence Nightingale horrified her parents when she told them she wanted to be a nurse: in the 1840s, nurses were coarse old women who were often drunk. However, she went ahead, and when she set up a training school for nurses in 1860, it became respectable.

ENTERTAINMENTS

Ellen takes Alice and John downstairs each evening at five o'clock to spend an hour with their mother. They talk and play together, and Alice recites a poem she has learnt or sings a song. Children were required to learn a lot of poems by heart as well as long lists of

historical dates and Latin verbs. Poems for recitation were usually rousing or patriotic, such as Felicia Hemans' *The Homes of England* and *Casabianca*, which begins "The boy stood on the burning deck . . ." Mr Smith looks in on them when he comes home from work. Alice and John have to be very well-behaved in the drawing room, which is packed full of breakable ornaments – they are also rather in awe of their father, which makes them shy and quiet.

Right: *"Samplers" like this were for practising the different stitches. They had the alphabet, a verse from the Bible, or a motto.*

Left: *Instructions for "tatting" – making delicate lace with a single cotton thread and a shuttle.*

Pastimes

Sewing was an important skill for Victorian women. If they were poor, it was essential that they knew how to make and mend clothes for their families, and if they were well-off, it was a suitable way to spend their leisure time. Mrs Smith does her sewing during the day, and embroiders while she is sitting with Mr Smith in the evening.

Scrap books were another pastime, and both adults and children would spend hours carefully pasting illustrations into albums with flour-and-water glue. They also made their own cards for birthdays and Valentine's day (*see illustration top left*). Pressing flowers and dried flower arranging were other favourite hobbies.

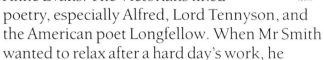

Above: *Painting was a hobby enjoyed by many. Queen Victoria spent her holidays in Scotland sketching and doing watercolours of the land surrounding Balmoral.*

Left: *The piano was almost a household god, and every drawing room had to have one. Girls were taught to play; one writer said it made them "sit upright and pay attention to details".*

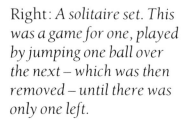

Other Amusements

The Victorians were great readers and diary-keepers. Mrs Smith, like many others, keeps a journal. Even Queen Victoria kept a diary and published extracts under the title *Leaves from a Journal of our Life in the Highlands*. Novels, which normally came out in monthly instalments in magazines like *Blackwood's*, were read by more people than ever before. Novelists would often be writing the section of the novel hours before it appeared in the magazine, with little idea of what was going to happen next. Some of the most famous authors were Dickens, Mrs Gaskell and Benjamin Disraeli, who was also Prime Minister twice (in 1868 and from 1874 to 1880). Although widely read, Disraeli's novels were not considered to be very good – the poet Wordsworth called them "trashy". Charlotte, Emily and Anne Brontë were also well known writers, as was George Eliot; because of the bias against women, the Brontës published their first books under men's names, and "George Eliot" was, in reality, Mary Anne Evans. The Victorians liked poetry, especially Alfred, Lord Tennyson, and the American poet Longfellow. When Mr Smith wanted to relax after a hard day's work, he looked at the cartoons in *Punch* magazine.

Right: *A solitaire set. This was a game for one, played by jumping one ball over the next – which was then removed – until there was only one left.*

ALBERT AT SCHOOL

A t six o'clock, while Alice and John were saying goodnight to Mr and Mrs Smith, their brother Albert was sitting down with his school friends for an evening meal.

Albert was sent away to public school when he was twelve. A public school is an independent school which charges a fee.

During the Victorian era, public schools came to be seen as the only ones which could give a "gentleman's education". It was important for a boy who wanted a good career to go to the right school, as it made it easier to get into either Oxford or Cambridge, which were considered the only universities suitable for gentlemen. Mr Smith very much wants Albert to attend one of these.

Public school education was thought to make boys into Christian gentlemen and natural rulers. Senior boys had a lot of power over younger ones, who had the job of "fagging" for them (cleaning their shoes, making their tea and doing other jobs of this kind). This was supposed to teach older boys to be good leaders, but sometimes it made them into bullies.

Above: *Young children practised writing and did sums on a slate with a special "slate pencil" which could be rubbed out afterwards.*

Left: *Many children went to Sunday school. A child's education was not thought to be complete without it. They were taught about Christianity and learned passages from the Bible by heart.*

In the classroom, teaching was mainly in the "classical" subjects of Latin and Greek. These two subjects were thought to be the best training for the mind. They were also favoured because they were not practical subjects, and therefore not related to the sorts of things lower-class boys needed to learn in order to get into a trade. In modern terms, it was not a very useful education, but the Victorians thought that a person's social position and moral outlook were more important than what they had learned at school. Besides classics, lessons included history, geography and mathematics. While it was not important to be top of the class, the boys had to work hard enough to pass the exams that were rapidly becoming the only way to get into a good profession.

Above: *A tennis racquet, hoop, leather ball and a "diabolo" or "devil on two sticks". The brown top was tossed up and caught on the string between the two poles.*

Left: *Older children who had mastered "copperplate" writing and simple arithmetic were given proper ink pens and exercise books. Each desk had an inkwell.*

Albert has a very different education from his sister Alice. Mr and Mrs Smith expect Albert and his younger brother John to have careers, but they expect Alice to marry and have children. As most girls were destined to be wives and mothers, it was thought wasteful to spend money educating them – some people even thought that too much studying made a girl ill. There were public day schools for girls in 1872, but they did not become popular until the start of the twentieth century. Oxford and Cambridge had colleges for women from 1869, but, while they were prepared to let "the petticoats" go to lectures and take exams, they refused to award them degrees for many years. Lower class girls learned to cook and keep house. Alice is thought not to need these skills because she will always have servants to do this work for her.

Right: *Both cricket and rugby were played at public school, as these games – unlike soccer – were considered suitable for gentlemen.*

DINNER

Smart people called their evening meal "dinner", and it was the largest of the day (servants called their evening meal "tea" and both referred to any meal taken later than this as "supper"). The Smiths always dress up for dinner, which never has less than four courses (not including cheese and fruit).

When Albert is home from school he joins his parents, but Alice and John eat in the nursery.

Left: Dinner is served when Jane bangs the gong at 8 o'clock.

Alcohol

Mr and Mrs Smith drink wine with their dinner. Afterwards, Mr Smith allows himself one glass of port. Mrs Smith has coffee.

Despite warnings about the "demon drink", drunkenness was a terrible problem. Alcohol was cheap – "Drunk for a penny, dead drunk for twopence" – and many poor people turned to beer shops and "gin palaces" to escape the misery in which they lived. William Booth of the Salvation Army tried to persuade people not to drink, and Thomas Cook, the famous travel agent, started his trips and excursions because he hoped they would keep people out of the pub.

"If I don't stand perfectly still when the master and mistress are eating, I have to come up before the mistress the next morning."
Jane Dobbs

Jane stays in the dining room during dinner to serve food and fetch anything that is wanted. Between courses, she brushes any crumbs from the table cloth with a silver crumb brush.

Dinner Parties

Dinner parties were a popular way of entertaining guests. There were two ways of serving dinners: either the food was laid on the table and the guests helped themselves, or they were each given a menu card and their choice of food was brought to them by a servant. This method was called *à la Russe* and it was considered very smart. Several different wines would be served with the meal, often including champagne. Punch was popular, as was "negus", which was made with port wine, hot water, sugar, lemons and nutmeg.

Mrs Cooper insists on a lot of advance warning if Mrs Smith invites people for dinner, because it means a lot of extra work. Mrs Smith values Mrs Cooper's excellent cooking, and tries not to invite dinner guests too often, in case Mrs Cooper gets angry and leaves.

MENU

Crimped Cod & Oyster Sauce
Fried Perch & Dutch Sauce

Pigs' Feet à la Béchamel
Curried Rabbit

Roast Suckling Pig · Boiled Fowls &
Oyster Sauce · Vegetables

Jugged Hare

Merangues à la Crème · Apple Custard
Vol-au-Vent of Pears

Dessert

Above: *Fancy moulds for jellies, blancmanges and puddings.*

Below: *Typical dinner dishes: mulligatawny soup, boiled beef and carrots, blancmange and fruit.*

Left: *Fashionable ladies and gentlemen at a dinner party.*

AN EVENING OUT

Mr and Mrs Smith sometimes go out in the evening to a friend's house for dinner, or a party or ball. There is plenty of other entertainment, however, and they also go to plays, concerts and operas. These are often held in the Albert Hall, built in 1871 by the Queen as a memorial to her husband, Prince Albert. Shakespeare is a favourite at the theatre, and operas range from serious classical ones to funny operettas by Gilbert and Sullivan. There are also music halls, but these are mainly for lower-class people and the Smiths would not think of going to one. Music halls have shows with comedians who sing and tell jokes. Some of the songs they sang, such as "Daisy, daisy, give me your answer do", and "My old man said follow the van" are still sung today. Many famous actors, including Charlie Chaplin, began their careers in the music halls.

The Smiths go out in their carriage but those with less money take the tram or train. Electric trams began to replace horse-drawn ones in the 1890s, and the first London Underground railway – the Metropolitan line – was opened in 1863. A hackney cab – the Victorian equivalent of the taxi – could also be hired.

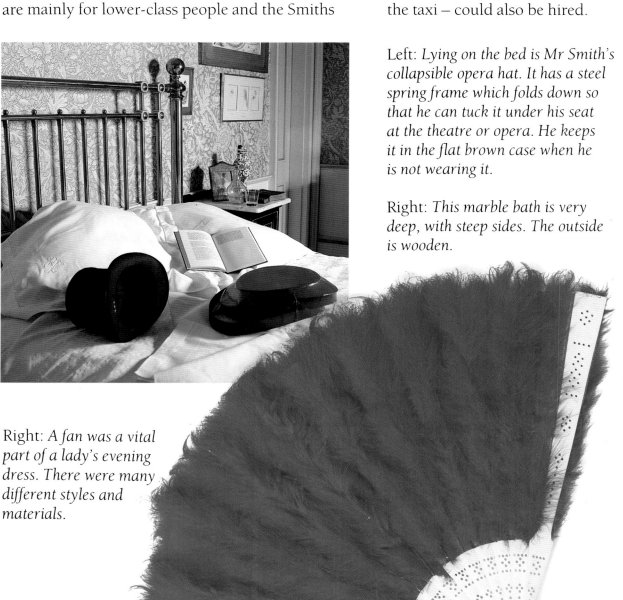

Left: *Lying on the bed is Mr Smith's collapsible opera hat. It has a steel spring frame which folds down so that he can tuck it under his seat at the theatre or opera. He keeps it in the flat brown case when he is not wearing it.*

Right: *This marble bath is very deep, with steep sides. The outside is wooden.*

Right: *A fan was a vital part of a lady's evening dress. There were many different styles and materials.*

BATHING

The Smith family bath every day, but like most people, they think that one bath a week is enough for their servants. Before Mr Smith had this bath (below) installed, Jane and Mary had to carry the tub up to the Smiths' bedroom and fill it up with hot water brought from

Left: *A baby's bath with a can for carrying water.*

downstairs. The Smiths would take their baths in front of a roaring fire, surrounded by screens to keep out the draughts. Although Jane and Mary are pleased about the new bathroom, they are not allowed to use it. They still have to lug their tin bath and water all the way up to their attic rooms. Although many water pipes and sewers were put down in the late Victorian period, conditions in the poor parts of cities were still bad: there were slums where one tap and one toilet were shared between twenty-five families who queued up to use them every morning. Problems with hygiene caused epidemics of cholera and typhoid – rich people got these illnesses as often as poor ones, and Prince Albert died of typhoid in 1861.

Above: *The Smiths had a water-closet like this.*

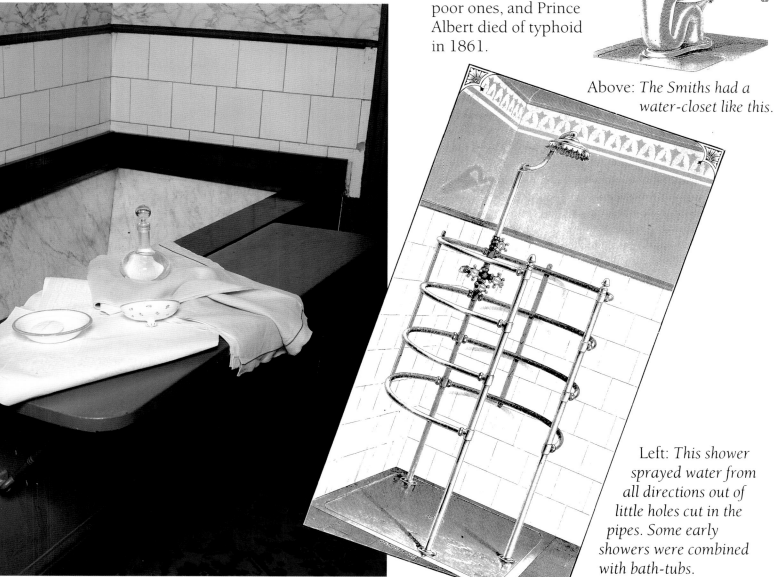

Left: *This shower sprayed water from all directions out of little holes cut in the pipes. Some early showers were combined with bath-tubs.*

BEDTIME

Beds were made of brass or iron, with feather-lined mattresses. Mr and Mrs Smith's night clothes are laid out neatly for them every night, and, if it is winter, a stone hot water bottle is put into the bed to warm it .

The Smiths and their servants all say prayers privately before they go to sleep. Like most other people, they go to church on Sundays and say prayers before meals. The vast majority of Victorians were Anglican and believed in a God who would "save" mankind, which was thought to be naturally sinful. The Victorians believed in helping those less well-off than themselves by charity and social reform, but they also believed that God would punish those who "got above themselves". This was especially true of servants, who were often told that their place was to serve their "betters" and that if they did it well, they would have their reward in heaven.

Right: *Snuffers for putting out the candles.*

Left: *Candles and oil lamps to light the Smiths and their servants to bed.*

Right: *Mrs Smith's dressing table.*

Left: *Clothes like this chemise had details which required hours of painstaking work.*

Nightworkers

There were many people who worked longer hours even than servants. Amongst these were seamstresses, who were very badly paid and often ruined their health and eyesight by sewing late into the night in poor light. The picture on the left shows a seamstress who has collapsed from exhaustion amidst the ruffles of the ballgown she is sewing.

Watchmen and policemen also worked at night. The police force was set up by Sir Robert Peel in 1829, which is why they were nicknamed "peelers" or "bobbies". They wore top hats and carried truncheons. They were especially important in big cities where there were many burglars and pickpockets.

The servants' rooms – usually in the attic – were drab and cheerless, with grey walls, bare floor-boards, lumpy mattresses and a chipped basin and ewer. Often furniture which was too old or scruffy for the rest of the house was put in the servants' quarters. When employers had gas and electricity put into their houses, most of them did not think it was worth extending the pipes and cables upstairs for the servants, so their rooms were often dark and cold.

Left: *A basin and ewer (pitcher) for washing were kept in each bedroom.*

"I must try to finish making my dress this week, but I have been so driven at work I have had hardly any time for myself. I do not go to bed till nearly twelve at night and sometimes I feel so tired I am obliged to have a good cry." Mary Parker

Above: *Chamber pots were kept under the beds in case people needed to go to the toilet in the night. They were emptied by the servants every morning.*

If the Smiths have any trouble getting to sleep they can ask one of the servants to fetch them some laudanum. This was a solution containing the drug opium, which Mrs Beeton recommended that everyone keep in their family medicine chest. Opium was so widely used for both adults and children that it has been called "the Victorian aspirin" (the aspirin itself was not invented until the 1890s). Doctors did not realize how dangerous opium was, although it was known that people who took it often became addicts. However, despite the occasional nuisance of "bed bugs", the Smiths usually sleep well, certain in the belief that their way of life will never change and that the sun will never set on the British Empire.

The House in Time

The Smiths moved into this particular house in 1875, and lived there until 1885, when they moved to a larger house in a more fashionable part of London. Here are some of the things that took place in Britain and around the world before, during and after this period, in the reign of Queen Victoria.

1837 Death of King William IV. Victoria, aged 18, becomes queen. American Samuel Morse invents the telegraph.

1838 The first practical photographic process is developed by Frenchman Louis Daguerre (early photographs are called "daguerrotypes").

1839 Chartist agitation for electoral reform leads to riots.

1839-1842 The Opium War with China.

1840 The penny post is introduced in England. The first postage stamp is the "Penny Black". Queen Victoria marries her cousin, Albert of Saxe-Coburg-Gotha.

1845 The potato famine in Ireland causes mass emmigration to the USA. Texas becomes part of the USA.

1846-1848 War between USA and Mexico.

1847 The American claim to Oregon country is recognized by Britain. After the famine in Ireland, the Irish revolutionary movement grows.

1848 Marx and Engels publish the *Communist Manifesto*. The world's first women's rights convention is held in New York. The gold rush starts when gold is discovered in California. Mexico cedes California, New Mexico, Arizona, Utah and Colorado to the USA.

1849 Harrods department store is founded in London's Knightsbridge.

1850 The English poet William Wordsworth dies.

1851 The "Great Exhibition" opens in London. It includes exhibits from all over the world. American Isaac Merritt Singer invents the first practical domestic sewing machine.

1853 The USA uses force to get Japan to open up its ports to foreign trade.

1854-1856 The Crimean War: France and Britain declare war on Russia and win victories at Balaclava and Inkerman.

1855 The first pillar boxes for letters are put up in London. Florence Nightingale goes to the Crimea to look after the wounded soldiers at Scutari.

1857 The Indian Mutiny: Rebellion against the British by native soldiers in Northern India is suppressed.

1859 Charles Darwin's "Origin of Species" outlines the theory of evolution.

The discovery of oil in Pennsylvania, USA, leads to the development of the modern oil industry.

1861 Abraham Lincoln becomes the 16th President of America. Prince Albert dies of typhoid. Grief-stricken, Queen Victoria withdraws completely from public life.

1861-1865 The American Civil War, which ends with the surrender of the Confederates (Southern states) to the Unionists (Northern states) and the abolition of slavery in America.

1862-1886 Unrest as the American Indians are expelled from their homelands by settlers.

1863 The first underground railway line opens in London.

1864 The Red Cross Society is founded to care for war casualties.

1865 French scientist Louis Pasteur publishes his "germ theory" of disease. President Lincoln is assassinated. Vice-President Andrew Johnson succeeds him. The "Red Flag" Act requires drivers of self-propelled vehicles such as steam carriages to have a man walking in front carrying a red flag. The maximum speed limit is fixed at 4 mph (2 mph in towns).

1867 Swedish inventor Alfred Nobel manufactures dynamite. Karl Marx publishes *Das Kapital*, a critical study of capitalism. The USA buys Alaska from Russia for $7,200,000.

1868 Unrest in Ireland: the Fenians aim to overthrow British rule.

1869 The Suez Canal is officially opened. The first trans-Continental railway in the USA is completed.

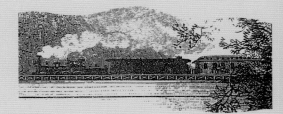

Ulysses S. Grant becomes the 18th President of America.

1870 Englishwoman Elizabeth Garrett Anderson is the first woman to qualify as a doctor. The English novelist Charles Dickens dies.

1871 The Irish "Home Rule" party is founded. Trade Unions are legalized in Britain.

1871 The first F.A. cup final is played in Britain: the Royal Engineers beat Crystal Palace 1-0.

1873 Remington Company begins to manufacture typewriters.

1873 The Smiths' house is built.

1876 American Alexander Graham Bell invents the telephone.
The Battle of Little Big Horn: American Sioux Indians defeat General Custer's troops.

1877 Queen Victoria is proclaimed Empress of India.
The first tennis championship is held at Wimbledon.
American Thomas Edison invents the microphone and the gramophone.

1877-1878 Russo-Turkish War. Romania, Montenegro and Serbia gain independence from Turkey.

1878 The Berlin Congress: Representatives from France, Britain, Germany, Austria, Turkey, Italy and Russia discuss the division of territory in Eastern Europe.

1878-1881 War between Britain and Afghanistan as Britain tries to secure its frontier in India against Russian advances into Asia.

1879 Thomas Edison invents the electric lamp.
The Zulus defeat the British at the Battle of Isandlhwana and are then defeated at Ulundi.

1878-1884 The War of the Pacific: Chile wins victories over Bolivia and Peru.

1880 Construction work on the Panama Canal begins.

1881 Electricity in houses and streets for the first time in Britain.
First Boer War: the British recognize the independence of Transvaal.
Anti-European riots in Egypt.
Tsar Alexander II of Russia is assassinated by terrorists' bombs. His son, Alexander III, succeeds him. He tries to stop the revolutionaries with harsh policies.

1882 British and French forces occupy Egypt to suppress unrest.
First commercial system of electrification put in operation in New York City.

1883 The Russian Marxist party is founded. Unrest follows.
British forces leave Egypt after an uprising. General Gordon and his garrison are massacred at Khartoum.
The first ten-storey "skyscraper" is built in Chicago, USA.

1883-1884 French expansion into Indo-China: after war with China, the French take control of Tonkin, Annam, and Cambodia.

1884 American inventor Hiram Maxim perfects the machine gun.

1885 German engineers Karl Benz and Gottlieb Daimler build a single-cylinder car and patent a gasoline engine.
The founding of India's first national political party, the Indian National Congress.

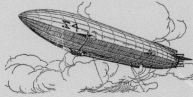

1886 Coca-Cola invented in America.
The first Home Rule bill creates a separate Irish legislature.

1887 Massive celebrations mark Queen Victoria's Golden Jubilee.

1888 Scotsman John Dunlop invents the pneumatic tyre.
American inventor George Eastman perfects his hand camera.

1889 The Eiffel Tower is built in Paris.

1890 The Battle of Wounded Knee is the last major Indian uprising in the USA.

1891 American W. L. Judson takes out the first patent for a zip-fastener.

1892 The English poet Alfred, Lord Tennyson dies.

1893 Keir Hardie founds the Independent Labour Party.

1895 German physicist Wilhelm Röntgen discovers x-rays.
Louis and Auguste Lumière show the first films to the public in Paris.
Italian Guglielmo Marconi invents the wireless telegraph.
American King C. Gillette invents the safety razor with throwaway blades.

1896 The maximum speed limit is raised to 14 mph.

1897 Queen Victoria's Diamond Jubilee: she is at the height of her popularity. There are shouts of "Go it, old girl!" when she appears on the balcony of Buckingham Palace to wave at the crowd.

1898 Dane Valdemar Poulsen invents the magnetic recording of sound.

1899 Aspirin is patented by the German company Bayer.

1899-1902 Second Boer War: the Boers accept British sovereignty in South Africa.

1900 German aeronaut Count Ferdinand von Zeppelin launches the first rigid airship.
The Commonwealth of Australia is created.
Austrian Sigmund Freud publishes his first work on psychoanalysis.

1901 Queen Victoria dies and her eldest son, the Prince of Wales, becomes King Edward VII.
Theodore Roosevelt becomes the 26th President of America.

GLOSSARY

Bed bugs Wingless, bloodsucking insects which infested Victorian homes. Although bed bugs were especially fond of dirty houses, they were a problem for everyone, including Queen Victoria who employed a special "bug-catcher" to deal with them. They were very hard to get rid of, but one of the more successful ways of dealing with them was to pour boiling water into the joints of the brass bedstead.

Bustle A padded frame used to bulk out the back of a skirt (*see page 14*). The bustle took over from the crinoline in the early 1870s as the means of creating the newly fashionable shape with the skirt straight in front but sticking out at the back. A special metal bustle was invented in the 1880s, which bunched up behind the wearer's bottom when she sat down and sprang automatically into place again when she stood up!

Chemise A one-piece undergarment for women, usually of a short, simple dress-shape, made of thin cloth (*see page 14*).

Cholera A short-lasting, often fatal infection caused by drinking or eating water, milk or food contaminated with bacteria. The symptoms are diarrhoea, vomiting and stomach pains, followed by collapse from loss of water and salt.

Colony A country and people which are controlled by another, foreign state — usually one which has invaded and conquered them.

Copperplate An ornate style of handwriting, so-called because it was modelled on engravings from copper printing plates (*see page 37*).

Corset An undergarment of cotton or wool made rigid by whalebones inserted into the cloth. Corsets were laced up tightly at the back so that the wearer's waist would be squeezed in and she would look slim (*see page 14*).

Crinoline A circular cage-like frame made of flexible steel wire hoops, worn underneath a skirt to give it a full shape (*see page 15*). Before crinolines were introduced in 1856, women had to wear as many as six full-length petticoats to make their skirts stick out in the fashionable bell shape. Crinolines were instantly popular because they were much lighter than layers of petticoats, and between 1856 and 1860 their hoops gradually grew larger and larger until skirts stuck out so far that it was impossible for two women to walk through a doorway together or sit down on the same sofa.

Drawers The Victorian equivalent of knickers for women. They were made of two separate "legs", joined on to a waistband (*see page 14*).

Drawing Room A formal room for entertaining guests. Drawing room is short for Withdrawing Room, and the room was given this name because the ladies of the house would "withdraw" to it after dinner to drink tea or coffee, leaving the men to drink port and smoke cigars around the dining room table.

Emery Paper Paper with a layer of a rough mineral powder known as "emery" glued on to one side (*see page 13*).

Frock coat A man's coat with knee-length "skirts" (*see page 16*).

Gaslight The first gaslight was yellow, smelly, smoky and very hot. Brilliant white gaslight was not made possible until the invention of special "incandescent" gas mantles in the 1890s. These were small hoods which were treated with chemicals so that when they were placed over the flame, it glowed more brightly than before. Electric lighting systems were being developed in the 1880s, but although electric lamps were popular in Britain by the end of the century, gas lighting was still the most widespread method (*see page 8*).

Hackney Cab A horse-drawn cab for hire. They were usually Hansom cabs, pulled by a single horse with the driver on a raised seat behind his passengers, who sat on lower seats with a hood over them to protect them from rain.

Jet A black stone (a form of coal), often used in jewellery-making. Most jet came from Whitby in Yorkshire (*see page 17*).

Mews A yard or street lined with stables and living quarters. Town houses such as the Smiths' were always built with a mews behind to house the occupants' horses and carriages. The living quarters were for carriage-drivers and grooms. Ownership of a carriage signified wealth and status, much as an expensive car does today.

Opium A drug made from the juice of the seed capsules of "opium poppies". It was popular in the last two centuries as a soothing medicine for calming people down and helping them sleep (*see page 43*). Opium was imported from India and British traders used it as a payment for Chinese goods such as silk and tea. Opium had been used as a medicine in China for many years, but the Chinese grew concerned about the growing numbers of addicts and tried to stop the trade. An Anglo–Chinese war broke out in 1839, ending in 1842 with China ceding control of Hong Kong to Britain. In 1857, a second war broke out, which also ended in a British victory. These wars were known as the "Opium wars".

Parlour A formal room, mainly used for entertaining guests.

Parlourmaid A senior maid who did not have to do the heavier work such as floor-scrubbing, but who performed tasks such as answering the door and serving food as well as cleaning. Servants had their own, very strict, "class structure". In houses with a large staff, the steward or butler was in charge, followed by the master's valet (the male equivalent of a lady's maid), the housekeeper, and the mistress' own maid. The lower servants had to wait on them, and address them as "Sir" or "Madam".

Range A stove, usually fed by coal or wood, with one or more ovens and a flat iron top with areas for heating up food in saucepans.

Reform Acts These were a series of acts passed in the nineteenth and early twentieth centuries to improve the fairness of the political system of England by giving more people the right to vote. The first important reform act was the 1832 act, which gave voting rights to all male property owners and householders who paid more than £10 in rent each year. This only included upper and middle class men, and a group called the "Chartists" was set up in 1839 to campaign for all men to be able to vote and stand as members of Parliament if they wished. The Chartists' campaign failed, but in 1867 and 1884 there were further reform acts that extended the vote to all male householders – which amounted to 28% of all the people aged over 20 in Great Britain. (In 1918, voting rights were granted to all men over 18, and women were allowed to vote for the first time, provided that they were over 30. The voting age for women was not lowered to 18 until 1928.)

Salvation Army An international Christian group organized along military lines. Founded in 1865 by Englishman William Booth, it performs charitable and missionary work among poor and homeless people (*see page 38*).

Sampler A small, decorative piece of needlework, often worked with different types of stitches (*see page 34*).

Screen This is a piece of moveable furniture used to give protection from heat or draughts. The one behind the baby's cradle on page 26 is called a "scrap screen" because it has been covered in paper cutouts which are coated with layers of varnish. This method of decoration was called "decoupage" and was very popular in Victorian times.

Slate A writing tablet, usually made from a smooth layer of slate in a wooden frame, used by schoolchildren (*see page 36*).

Suet Pudding A heavy, pale-coloured boiled pudding made from suet (that is, the hard fat from around the kidneys and loins of beef or mutton), flour, and either milk or water. Suet puddings can be sweet if treacle or marmalade is added, or savoury. Mrs Beeton recommended that savoury suet puddings be eaten with roasted meat or used as a crust for meat pies and puddings (*see page 25*).

Tuberculosis An infectious disease caused by the tubercule bacillus (a type of bacterium), which causes abnormal lumps to form in body organs, especially the lungs. The symptoms include fever, loss of weight, and a persistent cough, sometimes bringing up blood.

Typhoid A serious and highly infectious disease caused by bacteria. The symptoms are fever, diarrhoea, headaches and later, confusion and haemorrhaging of blood. Like cholera and tuberculosis, typhoid can be successfully treated nowadays, but in Victorian times these diseases caused many deaths.

INDEX

Please note: references to the Smith family are to be found under the headings 'father', 'mother', and 'children'.

PLACES TO VISIT

The following houses and museums have displays on aspects of Victorian life:

BEAUMARIS GAOL AND COURTHOUSE
Beaumaris, Isle of Anglesey, Gwynedd, Wales
Tel: 0286-679090

BYGONES AT HOLKHAM
Holkham Park, Wells-next-the-Sea, Norfolk
Tel: 0328-710806

CHURCHILL GARDENS MUSEUM
Venn's Lane, Aylestone Hill, Hereford
Tel: 0432-267409

THE GROVE MUSEUM
Near Ramsey, Isle of Man
Tel: 0624-675522

GUNNERSBURY PARK MUSEUM
Gunnersbury Park, London W3 8LQ
Tel: 081-992 1612

HUGHENDEN MANOR
(A National Trust Property, home of Benjamin Disraeli)
High Wycombe, Buckinghamshire
Tel: 0494-532580

D.H. LAWRENCE BIRTHPLACE MUSEUM
8A Victoria Street, Eastwood, Nottingham
Tel: 0773-763312

LINLEY SAMBOURNE HOUSE
18 Stafford Terrace, London W8 7BH
Tel: 081-994 1019

THE NEW LLOYD GEORGE MUSEUM
Llanystumdwy, Cricieth, Gwynedd, Wales
Tel: 0766-522071 & 0286-679090

OSBORNE HOUSE
East Cowes, Isle of Wight
Tel: 0983-200022

PRESTON HALL MUSEUM
Yarm Road, Stockton-on-Tees, Cleveland
Tel: 0642-781184

PRESTON MANOR
Preston Park, Brighton, East Sussex
Tel: 0273-603005 ext. 3239

PRIEST'S HOUSE MUSEUM
23-27 Hight Street, Wimbourne Minster, Dorset
Tel: 0202-882533

ROSSENDALE MUSEUM
Whitaker Park, Rawenstall, Rossendale, Lancashire
Tel: 0706-217777

THE SHAMBLES MUSEUM
16-20 Church Street, Newent, Gloucestershire
Tel: 0531-822144

THE TENEMENT HOUSE
(A National Trust for Scotland Property)
145 Buccleuch Street, Garnethill, Glasgow, G3 6QN, Scotland
Tel: 041-333 0183

Acknowledgements
Breslich & Foss would like to thank Sarah Levitt and Sharon Manitta from Gunnersbury Park Museum, Hilda Whiting from The Victorian Society, Adrian Morris, George Speaight, Munni Srivastava and June and William Wilson for their assistance.

Picture Credits

Bridgeman Art Library p.36 top centre.

Mary Evans Picture Library: p.4 bottom left, p.5 top right, bottom right, p.25 top right, p.29 top right, p.40 top centre.

Fine Art Photographs: p.8 top left.

Gunnersbury Park Museum: p.5 centre, p.7 bottom right, p.13 top centre, centre left, p.14-15 all photographs, p.16 centre, bottom left, p.17 top right, top left, bottom right, p.18 centre left, p.25 bottom right, p.26-27 all photographs, p.28 bottom left, top right, p.29 top right, p.31 all photographs, p.32 all photographs, p.33 bottom left, p.35 top left, bottom right, p.38-39 all photographs, p.40 bottom right, p.41 top left, p.42 top left, bottom left, p.43 top right.

Robert Opie Collection: p.28 bottom right, p.29 centre right, bottom right, p.34 centre left.

Royal Pavilion, Art Gallery and Museum, Brighton (Preston Manor): p.7 bottom left, p.13 bottom right, p.16 bottom right, p.20 top right, p.21 top left, bottom right, p.22 top left, top right, bottom left, bottom right, p.23 top left, centre right, bottom right, p.33 top left, bottom right, p.37 top right, p.42 centre right.

The Royal Collection © 1993 Her Majesty the Queen p.5 bottom left Windsor Castle. Royal Archives © 1993 Her Majesty the Queen p.17 bottom centre.

The Victorian Society, Linley Sambourne House: p.12 centre left, p.16 top right, p.19 centre right, p.20 centre left, p.24 top left, p.30 top right, bottom right, p.34 top right, p.40 centre left, p.41 bottom left, p.43 bottom left.